Manifesto of the Poor

Solutions Come From Below

Francisco Van der Hoff Boersma

Co-founder of Fairtrade

Permanent Publications

Published by
Permanent Publications
Hyden House Ltd, The Sustainability Centre, East Meon, Hampshire GU32 1HR
United Kingdom
Tel: 01730 823 311 Overseas: (international code +44 - 1730)
info@permanentpublications.co.uk
www.permanentpublications.co.uk

First French edition published under the title:
Manifeste des Pauvres: Les Solutions Viennent D'en Bas
© 2010 Francisco Van der Hoff Boersma

First English edition published in Canada under the title:
Manifesto of the Poor: Solutions Come From Below
© 2012 Just Us! Centre for Small Farms, www.justuscoffee.com
English translation by Jay Hartling

All photographs property of Just Us! Coffee Roasters Co-op
Published under licence in the United Kingdom and non-North American territories:
© 2014 Permanent Publications

Typesetting by Tim Harland
Cover design by John Adams
Cover image © Shyamalamuralinath / shutterstock.com

Index by Amit Prasad, 009amit@gmail.com

Printed in the UK by
Cambrian Printers, Aberystwyth, Wales

Printed on paper from mixed sources certified by the Forest Stewardship Council

The Forest Stewardship Council (FSC) is a non-profit international organisation established to promote the responsible management of the world's forests. Products carrying the FSC label are independently certified to assure consumers that they come from forests that are managed to meet the social, economic and ecological needs of present and future generations.

British Library Cataloguing-in-Publication Data
A catalogue record for this book is available from the British Library

ISBN 978 1 85623 170 1

In the midst of an economic crisis Father Frans van der Hoff asks us to occupy the market with solidarity and justice and create economies that work for people, not corporations. Creating living economies as part of Earth Democracy is not just possible; it has become necessary for peace justice and sustainability.

Vandana Shiva
Recipient of the Right Livelihood Award, Ecofeminist,
and author of several books including, *Earth Democracy*

Father Frans proposes that values and participation be relocated in their proper home – at the heart of a more humane and civilised economics. Moreover, in this report from the frontline, he demonstrates that the theory translates well into practice, with multiple emerging models and initiatives proving his point.

Jonathan Dawson
Head of Economics, Schumacher College

This little book packs a big punch. Father van der Hoff delivers a direct and provocative critique of the exploitation, violence and injustice that characterizes neo-liberal market globalization. He's equally straightforward in demanding respect and a fair deal for peasants and marginalized people. If you're not sure there is anything you can or should do to help, read this book. It will erase your doubt and rewrite your shopping list.

Nettie Wiebe
an organic farmer and Professor of Ethics
at the University of Saskatchewan,
former president of the National Farmers Union
and founding member of La Via Campesina

Weaving thirty years experience of working amongst the campesinos of Mexico with deep insights into the structural violence systemic in liberalism and globalisation, Father Fran's inspiring and thought-provoking Manifesto *offers us a practical and essential solution to the inherent inhumanity of capitalism: the solidarity economy, where people and Earth – and not the corporation – have the allegiance of those they feed.*

Mark Boyle
author of *The Moneyless Manifesto*

Fairtrade is more than an ethical shopping choice for a comfortable consumer class – it is the mechanism in which ecology and economy can meet, benefiting both our planet and its people. It brings dignity and worth to people throughout the world, and purpose to consumers who can significantly shape their society through their consumer choices. Father Frans explains why Fairtrade is a vital aspect for the development of an equitable, healthier human civilisation that also results in a more ecologically balanced world. The choice is literally in our hands and Father Frans' Manifesto *is an important template for everyone if we are serious about curbing economic and ecological collapse.*

Maddy Harland
co-founder *Permaculture Magazine: Practical Solutions for Self-Reliance*

Father Frans has reminded me of why I became a Fairtrade activist: for the establishment of the common good and the empowerment of the poor and marginalised. Thank you Father Frans for keeping us focussed on the real issues.

Greg Valerio
author of *Making Trouble: Fighting For Fair Trade Jewellery*,
founder of CRED Jewellery,
Winner of The Observer Ethical Awards Global Campaigner 2011

Father Frans' Manifesto *is forged in the Deep Mexico of Tehuantepec's indigenous communities. His trenchant insights on global capitalism and his passionate call for social justice are grounded in the praxis of the original Fairtrade movements.*

Eric Holt-Gimenez
Executive Director of Food First,
and author of *Food Movements Unite!* and *Food Rebellions* (with Raj Patel)

The New Internationalist *has long told the stories of cocoa, banana, tea and coffee farmers. More recently, it has worked with Fairtrade producers and has become directly involved by selling their goods. Frans'* Manifesto *is the perfect reminder of why we must continue to practice what we preach. Thank you.*

Michael York
The New Internationalist Co-operative

CONTENTS

THE AUTHOR

One of 15 children born into a poor farming family in Holland, Francisco Van der Hoff Boersma became a master strategist working on behalf of the dispossessed. After obtaining doctorates in theology and political economy, he went on to teach at the University of Ottawa. He still considers the University as an oasis for rest and support, but teaching was not for him – he wanted something more hands on.

He was drawn to the life of a 'worker priest' and chose to work in the mines of Chile where Allende's government had been elected with the hope of creating a just and caring society. It all came crashing down on 11th September 1973 with a *coup d'état* to overtrow Allende and his government. Frans was warned by a Captain in the army to flee to the border with just the clothes on his back and he went to Mexico where he sought refugee status.

After working with economic development projects in Mexico City for a few years, his Bishop asked him to evaluate what could be done for small coffee farmers of Oaxaca who were starving. There were innumerable obstacles to overcome in organizing hundreds of small-scale farmers into the Union of Indigenous Communities of the Isthmus Region (UCIRI) co-op. People who made good money acting as middlemen in the coffee trade felt threatened and accused co-op member of being communists. In concert with the government officials and the military, they did everything possible to discourage the co-op. 39 members of UCIRI were killed in the first seven years.

They persevered and today they are a model for other Fairtrade co-ops around the world and have an endless stream of people visiting to learn from their accomplishments in the isolated mountains of Oaxaca.

FOREWORD

As we celebrate 25 years of Fairtrade products on the shelves, we find a world reeling from economic crisis and teetering on environmental disaster. It couldn't be more timely for the co-founder of Fairtrade, Frans van der Hoff, to share his vision of an alternative future based on social solidarity. With trademark inspiration and uncompromising clarity of thought, he calls for an economy that puts smallholder farmers and the poor first in a globalisation based on solidarity among communities.

Van der Hoff sees Fairtrade as a kind of social laboratory. We have tried radical new ideas, and experimented with innovative ways of regulating trade, and we have found success – to the cynics' ever-lasting surprise – *because* we put people and justice first. Obviously, Fairtrade is not the answer to all the world's problems. And we know painfully well that we are just at the very start of a long and difficult journey. But Fairtrade does contain the seeds of wider, far-reaching change. This Manifesto is rooted in that practical experience of 'opposing and proposing', of respecting the ideas of the dispossessed and creating the living alternative.

Frans van der Hoff is a humbling role-model in his determination, following Gandhi's principles, 'to be the change you want to see'. Living with indigenous farmers in the mountains of Mexico, it is their reality which informs and colours his world vision. This book is neither a policy agenda for tackling poverty, nor a condescending Manifesto *for* the Poor. It is purposely a Manifesto of the poor – a wake-up call to the world to listen to the wisdom of the smallholder farmers and their call for a dignified justice. As he says, we should not look for solutions imposed from above; instead we should look to the organised smallholders, the marginalized indigenous, the poorest themselves for solutions.

This critique is sorely-needed. In the wake of the banking and financial crisis, it is truly shocking how fast the world has returned to business-as-usual. Public money and public institutions rescued banks and economies from a crisis caused by unfettered greed. And yet within the unabashed blink of an eye, mainstream policy-making has rushed to kneel again at the altar of the free market and the free pursuit of individualist gain.

Van der Hoff reminds us of the injustices and poverty engendered by capitalism and the urgent need for change. These crises, he argues, can help us realise what is not working well, and enable new ideas to blossom in the light of day.

This Manifesto is visionary, but never day-dreams. Fairtrade is grounded all too firmly in the messy complexity of reality for that. Creating an alternative economic model based on justice, seeking ways to put people and the planet first, is always challenging. Every step is deeply debated in the rough and tumble of moving the Fairtrade movement forward.

Yet Fairtrade has brought inspiration to people across the world. It has created a space to experiment in putting community first, working alongside disadvantaged smallholders, and focusing on the environment. That's why Fairtrade's popularity has soared, nowhere more so than in the Fairtrade Towns movement that has spread like wildfire across the world, bringing communities together on the local level while connecting them globally.

Frans van der Hoff calls on us all to continue experimenting, discussing and pushing movements for social solidarity, including Fairtrade, upward from below: organised producers, consumers and all those angry at the injustices that surround us. This Manifesto will surely add spark to that debate, and is the reminder we all need to pause in the rush and noise of our lives, think, listen – and act for change.

Harriet Lamb
Chief Executive, Fairtrade International

PREFACE

We can't just sit around waiting for a global solution.
Elinor Ostrum (1933-2012)
The first woman to receive the Nobel Prize in Economics, 2009

The Manifesto of the Poor is a very timely and an urgently needed example of development from the bottom up. It gives us the history and thinking behind the Fairtrade movement by one of its founders, Francisco Van der Hoff.

Francisco Van der Hoff is a Dutch worker-priest who earned doctorates in economics and theology. He was a *soixante-huitard* or student activist in Holland and then taught at the University of Ottawa before heading off to work in the mines of Chile and eventually the mountains of Oaxaca, Mexico with peasant coffee farmers, some of the poorest and most downtrodden people in the world.

Faced with the looming global economic free-for-all, or so-called 'free trade', in the 1980s, his idea was not only to protest but also to propose. The proposal of 'Fairtrade' was brilliant in its simplicity – farmers would organize into cooperatives; emphasize quality as well as social and environmental responsibility; build their capacity together; and go directly to market at a fair price. Previously, they had depended on middlemen, known as 'coyotes', to provide the required transportation, processing and marketing of their coffee. They were literally paid pennies per pound.

Of course it wasn't so simple to bypass these 'coyotes'. They were prominent and powerful business people who had friends in government and the military. It took tremendous creativity, perseverance and courage on the part of the small farmers but, seeing the first glimmer of hope for a better life for their families and communities, they risked their lives to challenge the status quo and many paid with their lives.

In Atlantic Canada, there's a similar story of the larger than life priest, Moses Coady, who worked with the poor miners, farmers and fishers during the Great Depression to help them organize themselves into cooperatives for the same reasons.

"You are poor enough to want it, and smart enough to get it", he would challenge them. There are obvious links between what became known as the Antigonish Movement, the development of liberation theology in Latin America, and consequently Fairtrade. It's a history of which Atlantic Canadians should be very proud.

Francisco Van der Hoff is very clear that Fairtrade is not about charity or making superficial reforms within our current economic system. He sums up his Manifesto when he says with deep conviction (and a twinkle in his eye) that: "Charity – and let's include international aid in this – is a form of bad manners invented by those in charge of the system to compensate for what could have been done". Fairtrade seeks to build an economy that gives dignity to all participants in the trade chain, from producers to consumers. It is meant to be a truly different way of doing business, based on solidarity between the people involved. Fairtrade also does not mean that everyone will aspire to a North American middle-class lifestyle. Van der Hoff is fond of saying that: "The big problem with the world is not poverty, but greed". He contends that we can live simply but with dignity if you have the basics: housing, food, health, education, and some control over your own future.

He challenges us to rethink our rather simplistic, linear, dog-eat-dog competitive practices which deny our common humanity and destroy our planet. How much longer can we cover up this destruction with token acts of charity and environmentalism and expect to survive?

Thanks to Francisco Van der Hoff for his great work over the years and for taking the time to articulate the thought behind it. Thanks to Jay Hartling for accepting the challenge of translation with enthusiasm. Many thanks to Kathy Day and Pat Salmon for their diligence in editing, layout and proofreading. And finally thanks to Pascal Gellrich for his assistance and encouragement from the start.

Jeff Moore MSW, LL.D(Hon), DCL(Hon)
Co-founder Just Us! Coffee Roasters Co-operative ,
Wolfville, Nova Scotia

INTRODUCTION

The Poor: Confronting the Economic Crisis

For more than thirty years I have toiled as a worker priest[1] in the mountains in the northern part of the Isthmus of Tehuantepec, in southern Mexico, with the Zapotec, Mixe, Chatino and Chontal peoples. Just like my campesino[2] colleagues and friends, I barely make enough to pay for my daily food. Working and living among the campesinos and farmers who grow coffee, corn, beans and fruit, I have realized that these people live in a permanent state of structural crisis. Their earnings barely reach two dollars a day.

Many people ask me in what way the current global economic crisis affects the lives of indigenous peoples. I am obligated to reply that a state of crisis is practically the norm in the mountains. It is in this context that they live, or rather, have *survived,* for centuries, although they have not allowed the crisis to crush their spirit. They are constantly searching for new ways to break from the crisis and carry on. Their way of life is inspired by the ancestral wisdom of campesinos that consists of a love of life, resistance and never losing hope. The exclusion that exists, and the exploitation and humiliation that they suffer does not result in despair, but rather in hope for a dignified life and the expectation of a way out. It is not the promise of struggle or of a revolution; but positive, creative thought that has nothing to do with the weak morality of humanism. For indigenous peoples,

---

[1]   Worker priest: a Roman Catholic priest who has full time or part-time employment in a secular job without depending on the church for income.

[2]   Campesino: a term used for a small farmer or farmer family in Latin America.

solidarity is the expression of the social essence of humankind itself; it is not just the sum of individuals.

Indigenous peoples do not expect much from the pure, rational sciences. I am not a romantic. Life in the countryside is extremely difficult. Despite having several doctorates in sciences, I have learned a great deal from their common sense and experience: to explore new pathways, to protest and at the same time to propose. The time has come to put human beings and all living things at the centre, the beginning and the end. The objective of this manifesto is to provide hope to all those who resist the destruction of life and the pathway to death. I have become a fervent advocate of the creation of a space for thought and analysis based in the ancestral practices of indigenous small farmers to recover collective and communal social space. I believe that another way of social organization is possible because capitalism is nothing more than the legal and systematic organization of injustice, inequality and exclusion – because existing democracies are fictitious. They are inventions that serve particular and private interests. Only those who have the means for these particular interests can survive – never the most vulnerable.

It is from this fundamental ability to survive that the idea of a social and solidarity economy was born some years ago. The social solidarity economy envisions a market where campesinos can benefit from the produce that they grow without being exploited; participate in the improvement of their environment; improve living conditions for their families; and, above all, organize themselves in production cooperatives so that the efforts, means and benefits are mutual. The re-establishment of organic agriculture arose from this vision and development of our own credit and loans cooperative and the creation of networks.

The alternative economy does not merely consist of the introduction of a social dimension in the existing world market system. It is above all a different vision. It is about all of us surviving on our planet, with the condition that we first recognize differences, and create rules that control the violent nature of the economy and the market. These are the indispensable foundations needed to improve the survival of indigenous communities. For this reason, we did not pursue foreign funding to develop our projects. Instead, we drew upon our own wherewithal, strength, time, labour and sweat. Similarly, we declined all charity, especially that which comes from above – from the wealthy. Charity, while aiding the poor and miserable of the world, is like a medicine that gets applied after subjecting them to violence and exclusion.

I don't believe in miracles, and even less in promises. That is why we have created our own pathways to improvement, self-sufficiency, food security and responsibility with respect to the lands that we have received from our ancestors. This has allowed us to create an efficient social enterprise, generate real added value to our agricultural products and commercialize them in the region where they are produced, exporting only our surplus, that which we do not consume, at a mutually-agreed-upon minimum price. This price is based on quality and a social premium always making it higher than conventional market prices. This enables us to maintain our customs, our culture and our social way of life. It has also enabled us to resist the threat of western individualism.

Beyond the indigenous communities in Mexico, where this entire adventure began, Fairtrade has taken on global dimensions that no one would have suspected at the start. In 56 countries in the South – among those, of course, is Mexico – the Fairtrade market was created based on an economy different from the ultra-liberal system, and it works! More than a million producers have benefited from Fairtrade. And, in 22 countries in the North, structures resulting from Fairtrade distribute the producers' goods. It is one of the few economic systems that functions without creating exclusion, and permits the poor to pass from the ranks of the excluded to being actors in an economy that does not seek to systematically harm them.

With this experience, I have one conviction: we can change the dominant system on a global scale. Even more importantly, the crisis that we have come to know in the last four years makes it all the more urgent to make that change. How will this happen? I don't know, but it will happen. The pressure from below is building, from those disadvantaged and abandoned by the current system. The poorest are increasingly questioning the current system. They want change and they want it now. This is the sense of history. Capitalism is far from being inherent in humankind. In fact, capitalism has only existed for 200 years and there is no doubt that its own contradictions contain the seeds of its inevitable evolution.

Fairtrade is one of the means to surpass the contradictions of capitalism. It acts on capitalism as a kind of catalyst or regulator. Do not look for another solution imposed from above by supposedly illuminated elites. The answer already exists – it resides in humankind, in its own capacity to resist, organize and fight. The poorest are not asking for anything. They have their own solution to capitalism, which is a system flawed and dying from within. The globalized world that is sold to us on a daily basis is only a myth. The new walls that are erected here and there by western countries in order to separate our different universes are evidence of this lie. I firmly believe that the organized poor can eliminate those barriers and walls of exclusion, and propose new paths to a better life together. We can't create paradise on earth, nor shall we, but isn't it better to daydream and to do what we can than to accept exploitation in darkness?

Chapter 1

THE PERMANENT STATE OF CRISIS

Cataclysmic Capitalism

What have we not heard, read or written about the global crisis? The most famous economists, historians, essayists and, of course, politicians have focused their words on hard globalization, the next September 11th which, unfortunately, promises the accelerated advancement of globalization. This, however, is the last stage of the death of cultures. The financial crisis has demonstrated the deep intrinsic instability of the western economic model, and above all the instability of worn-out neoliberalism. The evidence is there, and it is obvious: we must explore other avenues, but which ones? Very few voices are raised to propose concrete alternatives.

We must be aware: it is unlimited progress toward sustained growth and the world economy speeding toward a utopia that has brought us to our current situation. The crisis is already here. It is sowing a rage that feeds on the double sense of impotence and injustice. But the crisis is not only a financial crisis, or a crisis of the market, nor a result of the constant unjust distribution of wealth. It is also much more than a technical adjustment of the out-of-control liberal economy. While compassion grows for the victims – who make up more than half of humanity on the entire planet – no bold vision exists that provides clues to find a more profound solution. The massive injections of capital (the money of the citizens of northern countries!), and half-measures of all kinds, are not only insufficient, they don't cure the disease of the system once and for all. The crisis demands that we formulate new questions; it requires that we put aside the principles to which we are accustomed. It obligates us to undertake a profound and necessary questioning. We surely live in difficult times, but they are also exciting and promising. As Gramsci said, "the crisis consists precisely in the death of the old so that the new can be born ..."

In fact, it is increasingly clear that the primary causes of the malaise of modernity are individualism, the overemphasis, even the exclusive use, of rationality and self- serving organizations. People are essentially, and always have been, social and political beings. Among the deep corrections likely to better respond to the needs of society, only a true communitarian liberalism or liberal communitarianism, a real solidarity economy, could count on my support. From my point of view, this is essential to understanding where we are going. We have a responsibility to develop a social and solidarity economy. I am a man of hope, who is convinced that a different and better world is possible. However, there are a number of existing myths, economic and political lies, that we must first counteract and deconstruct before we propose new perspectives. The policies of hiding our heads in the sand are not justified. Mechanistic rationality on its own does not help us get our heads out of the sand. I think it is better to proclaim an end to thinking of this (neo-) liberalism as the only way to go. Former President of the UN General Assembly, Miguel d'Escoto, recently said, "The fall of Wall Street is, for the defenders of the free market, what the fall of the Berlin wall was to communism". This follows the words of Joseph Stiglitz: "The legacy of this crisis will be a global struggle of ideas and dreams to envision what might be better for humanity and the entire world". The first challenge of the crisis is not how to fix it. It is, rather, a profound questioning and the reconsideration of our traditional ways of viewing things. Over these last few years, all blame, and the origins of everything wrong with the planet, has been placed on the banks. In reality, they were useful scapegoats utilized in an opportune manner by the system to avoid broader questions. The banks did what they had to do: make more money. This isn't only greed; it is also obedience of the rules of the capitalist faith, and especially that of growth in order to survive. The concentration of power in the banks and corporations is truly dangerous. They are closely related and intertwined, much more than necessary. We have seen this – the breakdown in one leads to the breakdown of the rest.

The crisis first revealed itself publicly in the real estate and housing sectors. A small bank re-sold a risk to a larger bank and so on, until it reached Merrill Lynch, AIG and Lehman Brothers. However, when the system realized that the home buyers couldn't pay, it was too late and the entire structure collapsed, although it was predictable. They knew this was going to happen. The introduction of a law imposing a maximum price for a house or to authorize a maximum indebtedness would have sufficed. The problem is that in this sector, as in others, there are no price controls; nobody regulates supply and demand – only the desire to speculate. That is the problem of this free market: there are no controls.

Since we have plutocratic[1] governments, their interests are mixed with those of large corporations. That is why they don't do anything. Many banks that escaped control and did not respect rules of any kind – unless it was the dictatorship of maximized short-term profit – went broke or bankrupt. However, banks should organize themselves in order to minimize risks and avoid, for example, a borrower applying for a loan in order to pay

---

[1]   Plutocratic: government of, by and for the wealthy.

debt to cover another debt. They know that in the end, if too many borrowers do not pay the bank, the bank will end up in bankruptcy.

So why don't the same rules that apply to campesinos who are looking for a loan, or waged workers whose credit has a limit, apply to the big banks? In order to avoid all control and interference by the government, the big US banks that lost so much money in 2009 immediately repaid a large portion of the $700 billion provided by the Obama administration in the most severe part of the crisis. They managed to escape the rules that President Barak Obama attempted to enact in exchange for public financing. The President was right. After all, it was the public's money. Around the most severe time of the crisis, the head of Goldman Sachs declared, "I am only responsible to my company, not to the citizens". Nevertheless, he *is* responsible as a citizen and as an actor in the system. At the same time as the US government was handing out loans, it accumulated an overdraft that the citizens are now paying. None of this would ever have happened if the state had nationalized the banks and imposed the separation of retail banking and investment banking.

What is clear is that, in this crisis, to ensure that the system wins, no matter what, governments have continued to avoid the failure of capitalism. The current crisis is illuminating because it demonstrates that governments prefer to safeguard the existing system at all costs instead of seeking alternatives, because they are afraid of its demise. If the US government had not given $60 billion to Merrill Lynch, the bank would have disappeared, and, along with it, the entire banking system. Those who make economic decisions know full well that these are merely Band-Aid solutions that do not cure anything. On the other hand, since the state's cash registers are empty, if a new tremor were to occur soon, they would be devoid of any means to act. The damages caused by this savage or unbridled capitalism are incalculable. It is a type of cancer against which any kind of therapy cannot do much without causing some kind of electroshock in the organism.

In capitalism, there is a failure of civic responsibility, because nobody is guilty or responsible. It is always, in the end, the market that has the answer to everything. Market theories contain the following idea: the invisible hand or providence will fix everything, and the actors wash their hands of it. All this really depends more on a belief than on science. It is the belief in a divine providence. To doubt or denounce this axiom is considered sacrilege. The market opens a path to exclusion, violence, hate and death, in the sense that Freud and Keynes said talked about 'the death wish'.

The Failure of the God of Capitalism

Since the fall of the Berlin wall (so symbolic, and at the same time so real), the global psycho-political situation can be summarized with this formula: humanity has abandoned all intelligence, all critical sense, and has given priority to religion. The worst thing is that the religion of the unquestioned market dominates. However, we can and should propose a humane alternative to this dogma. In effect, current capitalism is a kind of alienation by religion – that of the liberal market, or the market prophet. Capitalism invented its own secular idiosyncrasy, and as such it has lost all moral horizons, the whole idea of eternity. It has been a disaster for all of humanity. Wealth and power are mounted on the throne of these fallen gods. Political discourse, propaganda and the media nourish them.

Though rather adverse to everything that relates to religion, capitalism has been able to give life to a whole set of beliefs that have their own providence, transcendent and imminent, present and absent, something which goes far beyond our imagination, but at the same time is in our brains and all our heads. The perversity of the system is based on a faith that claims that the selfish interests of individuals will naturally harmonize into the general interest, in a form of spontaneous self-regulation. But this supposed divine providence does not exist, and meanwhile, the problem of the allocation and distribution of scarce resources arises. Regardless, many people continue to believe that the market system, free from restraint and subject only to timid state laws, is regulated only by the famous 'invisible hand' made popular by the true theologian of capitalism, Adam Smith.

The mantras of ultra-capitalism, 'laissez-faire, laissez-aller',[2] free trade, 'without limitations' lead to colossal and disastrous consequences. Unfortunately, we have observed this quite recently. Liberalism has a dark and perverse side that is present even though we don't truly realize it. It is not based on a principle of regulation of human relations; it is based on a transcendental faith, a pagan providence guided only by profit and power. Blind faith in this god prevents us from seeing the reality of capitalism as it truly is: like a god. We believe in capitalism, without really knowing who it is, or where it is, where it is going and what it is really seeking. I can't say for certain what it really is. Scientifically, I cannot prove that it exists. Einstein said, "Maybe we understand 1% of how our universe functions, but we are only a tiny planet, in a gigantic system." So, how can we try to understand how the

---

2   Laissez-faire, laissez-aller: Literally translated mean 'let it be, let it go' – an economic doctrine that does not want government regulations and interminglings beyond the minimum necessary for a free enterprise to operate according its own economic laws.

system sustains itself as a whole? It is the belief in capitalism that
sustains it.

Thomas Hayek and Milton Friedman were fully aware that they
didn't have proper scientific arguments to validate the neoliberal
system. They said on various occasions, "We have to trust the
system in order for it to work! Why would we have more faith in
this system than any other? Are there no other alternatives?"
That's a big deal! That is why I label the crisis as a 'gift from God'.
We can finally open our eyes and convince people to leave
behind the ignorance that has maintained their uncertainties,
and progress toward knowledge, and therefore, more real science.
The providence of the liberal market is pure invention. It creates
the illusion that enables the excluded, the poor, campesinos and
beggars to believe in promises of progress, disguised by a
dangerous discourse that defends a 'fight against poverty'.
"Sleep well, people, even though your stomach is empty, the
market and its growth will ensure your future ..." Thomas Hayek
and Milton Friedman could have said. If this isn't a promise of
the same order as the paradise promised by religions, then what is?
In reality, liberalism is presented as a new god, with its power, its
omnipotence; as if it could do everything, regulate everything.
We are then confronted by a new type of myth. The problem is
this new god is far from making good on its promises, its divine
promises.

Poverty is Not a Curse

Since the events of 1989 – symbolized by the fall of the Berlin
wall – social and cultural confusion reigns on the face of the
planet. Nobody really knows for sure how fast or in what
direction the business world is taking us. They guide our steps.

Mediocrity is the rule. The selfish and their illusions have seized power. And, in politics, the deception that translates to permanent lies triumphs – at both the ideological and economic levels. The culture of narcissism is considered a good. Here, as well, resides the drama of the modern left that defends infinite progress for the entire world. It mirrors the messages from the business and political leaders 'above' and is in singular contrast with the reality of the ones from 'below'. This belief in modern capitalism has penetrated our heads and shaped development agencies, including NGOs. The very ideas of progress and economic development are sacrileges for the poor and the environment. Globalization leads its retinue of one-thousand-and-one-headed monsters, in the form of multinational and transnational companies, and has assured us that they are going to 'fix the world's problems'. Poverty? They promise to eradicate it by financing communications and promotional campaigns on glossy paper. They even support international institutions like the UN, to make poverty their '3rd millennium priority'. As such, they ridicule the reality of the poor.

As for me, labourer and member of a small community of coffee growers, my four doctorates have not absolved me from manual labour. Walking beside the small producers is onerous, hard and painful; but it is also a lesson of life, freedom and happiness. Because what they are seeking is not to become rich, but rather to live with dignity and, above all, escape from misery. For them, poverty is not a curse. That is what the campesinos of the mountains where I live and work have taught me for more than thirty years. It is important to provide a vision of hope and not block their horizon with a wall of confusion. Their resistance for struggle and survival, to earn their daily bread, opens new perspectives, although at times it is difficult to understand.

Nonetheless, the dominant opinion in the world is that we have to fight against the poor because they are potentially dangerous – the real potential terrorists. Besides, they don't consume anything and they do not contribute to the growth of rich countries. The large part of development aid provided by industrialized countries to the third world is based on this fear or concern, often unconscious, which makes it even more serious. The very notion of the war-like expression 'combat poverty' is based primarily on fear of the poor. For example, I recently had a document in my hands that summarized the development assistance policies of a government where you could read very clearly: "We should concentrate our aid in countries that are most likely to experience social instability..." in other words, revolution. It's frightening, isn't it?

Nevertheless, the capitalist system itself has created and nourished poverty and misery. They did not fall from the sky. Indeed, we often forget that capitalism's birth was accompanied by colonialism, and without it, it would not have been possible. Capitalism was fed on the riches confiscated from the countries of the south. That is how poverty appeared. With the 'discovery' of America, Africa and Asia, the explorers and colonizers inventoried all of the wealth so that they could later remove it from the earth and its inhabitants and export it to the countries in the north. In doing so, they destroyed entire cultures and indigenous forms of government, which had the effect that entire peoples were ungovernable until recently, unless they were governed by military or corrupt governments.

The first demonstration of conscience by the exploited was the American Revolution that began in Boston, during the famous Boston Tea Party. The English had a monopoly on all tea coming from the Indias and this tea was the principal beverage in the New World. The inhabitants, driven by rising taxes and the abuses of the settlers, rebelled and threw entire shipments of tea into the ocean. It was the first reaction by Americans that demonstrated to the English masters that they did not want to be their slaves. It ended in the first revolution of modern times. Although the Americans later repeated the imposition of new slavery on Africans, the episode is enlightening in terms of the violence that constituted the beginnings of capitalism.

No, poverty does not fall from the sky. It is neoliberal capitalism that produces it, and society that wants it. The accumulation of wealth without boundaries in rich nations creates poverty itself. There is a mathematical correlation between the two. Since resources and assets exist in limited quantities in the earth, what fills the pockets of one has to come out of the pockets of another. I am not against profit, but we must control its division and redistribution. What is at stake is the 'democratization' and redistribution of profit. For example, we must establish regulations that prevent an employer from earning 200 times the amount of the lowest wage paid to his employees or workers. I dream of the day when the democratic state proposes fairer regulations for sharing revenue: a certain amount for social programs, some for investment, a certain amount for ecology, a certain amount for workers and a certain amount for shareholders. Meanwhile, only the shareholders get to decide and take everything, and we can see where it leads. Yes, we should reward risk, but not at 20%. It would be enough at 3-5% to pay for the risk taken by capital; that would be equivalent to the rate of return provided by the average bank savings account. Why does capital need such a high rate of return?

Capitalism created a particular climate. All of its actors are related in an inextricable manner, and all of its satellites soak in a bath of dependency. In this context, the purpose of Fairtrade is to act as an instrument or vehicle to mature the conscience. It acts to withdraw faith in the system and to lay it bare. Fairtrade will help the poor until everyone has become fully aware of reality. Many people trample on the dignity and justice, even the very existence of the poor, but little by little they will discover that the poor did not appear on their own. The system has created and segregated the poor and kept them in misery. At this time, we continue to produce poverty. We must find solutions to put an end to it, and entrust ourselves to a different market because we suspect the failures of today's capitalism, which are enormous failures, especially from the point of view of the excluded. However, we must be careful in this crisis. Fairtrade must keep its distance from the dominant system, otherwise it will become part of its confinement.

We are all Responsible

One would have imagined that the causes of the crisis and its analysis had taught us some reforms. Unfortunately, there has been none of this, and we have learned absolutely nothing from the supposed lessons of the crisis. In fact, it has been the opposite. Even though they failed in the face of the entire world, the ideas and ideologies that have sustained the system are fighting back with full force. To get out of the crisis, they relied on the state and public money, which is acting contrary to their economic dogma of minimal government interference. In doing so, they converted private debt to public debt. They consolidated the idea that it is normal to privatize benefits and socialize losses – a peculiar way of affirming their belief in the market and capitalism as a social system. That is no longer capitalism, it is banditry. Moreover, the advocates of the neoliberal matrix dropped their financial burden, and threw it on the shoulders of the entire populace, who, for the most part, had nothing to do with the origins of the actual crisis.

The worst thing is that liberalism continues to promote an illusion, that it has led to positive achievements: the rise of individual liberties rather than multiple forms of slavery, the rise of technological progress, and the production of goods and services without precedent. However, there is one major problem that it has not resolved: the poor distribution of the fruits of these efforts, and the goods and wealth derived from them.

On the one hand, the current crisis has brought to light the strength of Fairtrade. On the other, it reveals that the goals of the liberal economy are to globalize everything, not only economic power, but also ideological power, imposing its vision and perception of life, individualizing everything and leaving the social to the private level, when it is not completely suppressing it. I am not against globalization; I would like to globalize Fairtrade. However, I have many reservations about the models that are proclaimed from above. The real question is to know what is meant by globalization, because in reality it is not just economic. There are other hegemonic goals like extending the model of western democracy everywhere, and promoting an individualist culture. This would result in the homogenization of everything. Suddenly, we are all on the same train, without wanting to be there. But at the same time, there is resistance. Globalization is an obsession of the market, as it has been in all systems. However, globalization abuses cultures and differences; it ruins diversity and results in the singular model of globalization. So, I propose *de*-globalization. This does not mean that I am against globalization, but rather, a globalization of solidarity and social organizations.

In the midst of all this, the poor and the excluded would prefer a model that respects and values their specificities and diversities. I believe we must learn from them. I also believe that exporting differences is better than importing a single model. It is what I refer to as the economy of dignified poverty. It takes into account the social and environmental costs of the growth dogma, because Fairtrade is an ecological system. Despite the crisis, the belief that eternal development without limits is possible continues to dominate. However, this belief has no scientific foundation. We know well that all growth has a detrimental effect on others and on the planet itself. The northern countries want to develop even more, although they have everything – perhaps too much. People are obese; they are easily bored and now they want to travel to the moon. Meanwhile, 80% of the rest of the world's population only wants to survive with dignity, that's all – and this survival has a relatively low cost. Even worse, is that we have realized that today, the countries of the south are suffering the consequences of global warming created by the countries of the north. Essentially, the northern countries are responsible for climate change. It is they that should ensure the protection of natural reserves, of resources and the environment. Before they tell neighbouring countries what to do, they should clean up their own backyard. The countries of the north have no right to tell the south that they cannot develop infrastructure because it will cause pollution. Why would they prohibit China from developing in the same manner that the West did in the past? The colonial powers have contaminated the world for centuries. On what basis may we prevent emerging countries from doing the same thing? Clearly, at the same time that China and India are developing in the same way as western countries, the planet is collapsing, but it is up to them to choose. The worst thing is that contrary to what we hear from all sides, China understands the importance of the environment. In the latest central government plan, the most important chapter deals with the environment. To some extent, they are also mobilized and know they must do something, although, on the other hand, they take actions that have irreversible consequences for the planet.

Despite the crisis, northern countries are unwilling to resolve the problems. All of them are responsible, not only Al Gore, who, by the way, admitted his mistakes. We must take the problems of the environment into greater account, but we must also resolve the problems of exclusion and exploitation. The polluters should pay: all chemical products or pollutants should be taxed. I know this is unrealistic, but nevertheless, it should be done.

Happiness? What is it?

Dignified poverty is the guarantee of having access to the basic things in life: land title, work, and fair remuneration to feed and maintain one's family; to have a solid home and basic infrastructure, such as access to healthcare and education. Each state should provide these things for its citizens. It would provide the guarantee for the poor to create democratic conditions for survival and to finally have the hope of a humanistic survival. To reach this point, it is necessary to find new criteria for measuring the happiness of society. Happiness is not for sale, and it cannot be bought. Food, life, health and education are the basic needs of every society. What more do we really need? The rest are just false necessities – artificial things that capitalism has imposed as goals for the entire world. It has produced a generation of idiots that have withdrawn to their keyboards and joysticks, busy with virtual war games. What stupidity! This illustrates the limits achieved by our ultra-violent society, like the success of the film Avatar. So much hate, but nevertheless so many viewers and so many awards ... Where is the poetry, the true life in all of this? We have lost the pleasure and value of things. Being together, being connected to one another, humanity has lost all of this. We have lost the social bond that binds us together. Even silence has ceased to exist. It is urgent that we adopt new ways of relating to each other that do not only happen through the internet, video games and shopping centres. It is urgent that we develop eco-tourism regulated by campesinos themselves, movements that advance ethical and organic eco-gastronomic food, and return to contact with nature, take the time to appreciate everything around us, like the birds, the forests ...

Liberalism has generated neither individual liberty nor social responsibility: today, there is a scarcity of everything in contemporary societies: in churches, unions, states. Leaders' declarations multiply, but they don't do anything, and therein lies the problem. Individual freedoms are not an end in themselves; they only have meaning when they are subordinate to the interests of the collective. Today everything is permissible – I don't believe that is healthy. In Kenya, the Massai are grouped together in little villages under the pretext that it is to better protect them, but in reality it is to control them. Meanwhile, thousands of hectares of their land are sold to multinationals so they can produce food for North America or Europe. It is an aberration. It makes me angry that there is no state authority that does anything about these absurdities or anomalies. In the best of cases, it demonstrates the irresponsibility and incapacity of governments, but also their lack of political will. There are fundamental things at the anthropological level; people want to be acknowledged as human beings, not as a beasts or slaves. This implies certain rights: the recognition of different ways of life, of their environment, different states of humanity. Parallel to this, there is a reversal, particularly in the countries of the north: with feelings, rationality, establishing social ineptitude, the denial of beings … even though, according to nature, we are social beings. We are in denial of the human being.

In a world where mediocrity reigns, where we think no further than our noses, and while the crisis forces us to completely deconstruct the capitalist system, the obvious path is hidden. It is not easy to propose something new, but it is urgent that we do so, multiplying experiences, communicating and engaging in dialogue with each other. Fairtrade allows the consumer the possibility to be a reflective actor in his/her own purchasing decisions, beyond any propaganda and any conditioning. This implies a willingness to leave the mania of the ego-herd mentality in which we are increasingly enclosed. Buying Fairtrade products is a demonstration that another world is possible.

The State Scares Me!

The poor of the world are furious and demanding the introduction of clear rules in the financial world and the markets – to have limits. They are also aware that the tap on the financial jacuzzi must be turned off and certain social and humane rules imposed. One might as well scream in the desert. They are asking this of weak states whose economies are mere shadows of the economy that developed during the period of deregulation from 1990-2000. States have been reduced to merely safeguarding the system and trying to recuperate whatever they can. There are no longer any states that exist that are managed in a democratic manner, only in a plutocratic manner. It is the banks and the big industrial and communications corporations that indirectly control the state. With feet and hands tied, manipulated by interests with greater powers, they are unable to enact profound change, so they cover the leaks as quickly as they can, and multiply the patches that they already know are ephemeral. Under the knife of ultra-liberalism, state responsibility is more and more limited, and unable to introduce a more social, fair economy. Still, isn't it the essence of a state to represent the entire population in a democratic manner, and to embody a kind of greater partnership of the interests of all and a form of consensus? And in theory, this works: territorial protections, the safety of citizens, the construction of infrastructure, are tasks that even the most liberal recognize as state responsibilities.

In reality, though, things happen differently. States are not truly democratic. Why was it that, in the USA, Barack Obama could not do what he wanted to ensure that a healthcare law was enacted? Because the large companies and their lobbies rebelled and in the end, they have more power than the president. The modern, plutocratic state is incapable of imposing rules, of controlling the banks, the stock market and multinational companies because it would go against the very people that put them in office. With Fairtrade, we are asking the state to finally take its social responsibility. What kind of food security do states propose for their citizens? What level of pollution is acceptable on the planet? What infrastructure will be guaranteed for all, particularly the most dispossessed? Leaving our fate and our future in the hands of private interests will not work in the future, as it did not work in the past. Or it will only function at the margins, where it can take advantage, as now happens, with concessions for highways or soccer stadiums. In some places, there will be wind turbine parks, because private companies that can exploit the opportunity with the support of the state, at a very low cost, will be able to sell the electricity they generate and make money – after expropriating the area from the owners of the land. In some countries, like Italy and Mexico for example, information media has been completely privatized. Why has the state not retained the ability to provide information to its citizens? How do we restore democracy? How do we create a state that truly represents different national interests and not those of only one group?

Faced with only plutocratic, manipulating and secretive states, the political choice is far from obvious. The parties that hold onto power want to keep it. Power has deaf ears with respect to the manifestation of null votes – either blank or a protest vote. Proof that this system doesn't function is provided in a democracy when a politician is elected with far less than 50% of the vote, and nobody cares. There is a great void in the functioning of states. Fairtrade tries to fill this void beginning with the democratization of the economy. By creating organizations based on majority mechanisms, and connecting them, the poor develop their consciousness and give rise to the feeling that in the end power can be in the hands of the people. It remains to be proven.

Chapter 2

GLOBALIZATION FROM BELOW

Growth ... What for?

I am inclined to think that the global financial and economic crisis is the expression of the defects of ultra-liberal capitalism and its violent character, but at the same time, the actual crisis is a challenge. It is like the eruption of a dormant volcano that finally spits out the sediments that have been hidden for years below the earth's crust. However, there are good volcanoes and bad volcanoes. Some eruptions contribute to a new fertility. In this case, the crisis that we know is the spark that ignites the system. We have to work hard and without rest to find decent and human alternatives to this hell. The tragedy is such that the bill for the damage must be paid by the poor, the most dispossessed families, abandoned communities and future generations. This is not tolerable.

Up until now, western domination ensured 'the domain of truth' and could impose the belief in capitalism upon the entire world. However, for a long time the excluded, that is 80% of the world's population have been skeptical. It is this massive reservoir of poverty around the world today to whom we turn for other possible models.

The accumulation of problems caused by capitalism has given rise to the need to change the matrix. Fairtrade is like a thorn in the back of capitalism creating a reaction, like a swelling that will subside. It prompts us to change the rules and question capitalism from the inside, including its dogmas, such as the one of unlimited development.

The idea, commonly accepted and shared, that development is a wonderful thing that is drawn from scientific progress and promises eternal growth is an absolute myth. Nonetheless, it is the most harmful evil that has been unleashed on humanity, because in fact, the planet and its resources are finite. Why constantly be persuaded otherwise? Every day, more and more, the planet demonstrates its limits. It cannot take it anymore. The resources and money that arrive in one place necessarily originate in another. The wealth of some irrevocably causes the impoverishment of others. The growth of poverty demonstrates that unlimited progress does not exist. It is pure fiction. Everyone in the world knows that global warming exists and that it is a virtual hell produced constantly by pollution. Positivism assured us that with science the future was bright and that nothing could detain progress. At the same time, we do not worry about social issues, or the environment, or the unemployed.

The system has left numerous scapegoat victims at the side of the road. It feeds upon them. They are indispensable for its existence and development. It is in the victimization of those who have nothing that the system finds its justification. The system proclaims human rights, like the right to life, to work, to dignity and housing, but it is incapable of respecting those rights. To defend itself, capitalism claims that when growth returns or improves, there will automatically be work for the poor, and this will end their misery. We must end, once and for all, this blind faith.

In fact, the accelerated development of the 20th century capitalist world was based on the exploitation of two-thirds of the planet and its population – the poor who suffer, the poor, who only want a life, never mind a *better* life. Having a roof over one's head, a house, a latrine, a stove, that is not even development. They are just necessities. In the same vein, attending school and improving your education and learning of the world is essential. It is true that development contributed to benefits, but we haven't measured the disadvantages. Science and individual liberties are all well and good, but at the same time that the north was developing, it was stealing wealth from the south. We must be honest and recognize that development could only have happened that way. It is, therefore, a completely fictitious construction. It is true, in the scale of human history, that the concept of development is relatively recent, even in western culture. We have to de-fetishize and demystify this idea that the economy always progresses for the better – good year or bad year – because the cost of the damage it causes to people and the earth is colossal. We are talking about human beings and our small planet, the only place we have to live. Globalization and corporate relocations are new forms of colonialism. Northern countries take advantage of cheap labour in order to produce goods for their consumption. The engine of capitalism is the exploitation of people by people. Why does the north insist so much in the development of the countries of the south? Because they need consumers to consume their imports! Development and its problems should be understood as an element of western thought that believes it should continue indefinitely. In this way, development contrasts with underdevelopment like a dichotomy that rests upon a semantic illusion. Development can only exist if there is a constant creation of underdevelopment and as such, creates the illusion that someday, and in the same manner, all underdeveloped countries may be materially prosperous. A second substantial illusion conceals the fact that development can only happen thanks to the constant exploitation of resources that are in no way inexhaustible.

The liberal economy creates more rights for some – for example banks – than for others. Thirty percent of North Americans who live below the poverty line in this affluent society can testify to this. It seems incapable of solidary. How can we create decency, solidarity and responsibility? How can we assert that we all have the same rights? We are not angels; we cannot create heaven on earth. However, the idea is to try to decrease the rate of exploitation in everything we do. So, we created a Fairtrade network to rescue the weakest, those who are denied basic rights.

No to Charity

In the capitalist system, those who accumulate wealth and power at the same time express, albeit unconsciously, a repentance for leaving the poor to one side. That is where charity comes from. Charity – put on the same level as international aid – is a perverse way, imagined by the defenders of the system, to compensate what they could have done in the first place – pay for labour and primary materials at a fair price and cover the cost of production. Charity in the market is harmful, because it denies that the poor are also human beings, subjects with rights. It instrumentalizes the poor as objects, as North Americans have done to the victims of the earthquake in Haiti. It gives the appearance of emergency humanitarian aid to the political aim of taking advantage of a crisis to promote their interests. As Naomi Klein writes, "In periods of extreme crisis, people are sufficiently desperate to take humanitarian aid of any nature, financing in any form, and they are not in a favourable position to negotiate the conditions of this aid". This does not preclude solidarity with the people who suffer when there are natural disasters, as with the Haitian people. However, it is the form and the conditions of solidarity that make it acceptable or not.

Charity treats the other as an object, not as a subject or living being. This demonstrates the incapacity of the actual system to sustain life. Begging for money is the most humiliating thing that exists in the world. The system of development from the north to the south consists of saying 'here is the money'. It is so humiliating that one cannot accept it. It is a form of neo-colonialism that seeks to take wealth and raw materials and convert the masses. This brutal capitalism has the same values. Through this system, the north still tries to impose its vision, its concept of development and its abstract humanism, in the disguise of sustainable development. The west never asks the colonized what it is that they want – ever. However, hidden wealth exists in the world that the system does not accept, values that it ignores. Daily resistance and survival create a popular wisdom amongst the most disadvantaged that is ignored or mistreated in the dominant culture.

Their desire to control their own destiny is normal. It is expressed in a cry that is translated by Fairtrade. Their actions act as a stone in the neoliberal shoe. Fairtrade allows them to exercise their own capacity and do what they believe is best for them, because they know perfectly the burden of exploitation. It is not scientific, it is something within. For this reason the campesinos reject the false equilibrium that is imposed by an inequitable market. Why would they do more to be further exploited? Simply put – they want to live with what they need, that is all.

First and foremost, the cost of the labour of a worker would have to be recognized, instead of providing gifts to pacify them, in the form of donations or subsidies, always with their hidden ideologies that 'at least we are doing something for the poor'. This has nothing to do with solidarity. It is essential to pay the poor better so they can buy what they need instead of relying on the assistance of NGOs (non-governmental organizations). From my point of view, international aid in all its forms has numerous disadvantages. Often, the NGOs show up in southern countries in conquered territory knowing better than the residents what is good for them, without asking the poorest what it is they need. They always combine their donations with rules that are invented on the fly, imposing their will on the people under the guise of charity. I do not approve of the actions of NGOs because they do not know what they are doing. You will find among their ranks people who are very sympathetic, competent, and full of good intentions. However, generally-speaking the machinery around them functions in reverse of what should be done. The mechanism of NGOs is the weapon of mass destruction that justifies the liberal system. NGOs function in long-term programs and projects whose priorities are dictated by the donors, and not by function of local needs. How many projects have I seen that have been implemented and then disappeared in three to five years, without anyone worrying about what would happen after that, and without passing the baton to anyone? The most common occurrence is that NGOs all intervene at the same time in the same place without any collaboration. What they are trying to do is lift the carpet of misery to publicize themselves. Problems must be studied and understood before coming up with solutions, and those solutions, like Fairtrade, come above all from the poor themselves.

Where I live in Mexico, the campesinos, dependent on coffee as their only cash crop, organized themselves because they were being exploited by middlemen and could not feed their families with the products of their labour. Still, certain intermediaries tried to choke them. However, it took some time for the campesinos to get organized. They wanted to do it in an independent manner, without state subsidies or external aid, to rediscover their dignity. They did not want to owe their shirts and pants to a government that underestimated them and did not respect them. And I, who share their lives, understand, because I have been living among them for many years. It is in this way – alone – that they have achieved their rights and have been heard, without selling out and without losing their soul. Thanks to Fairtrade, the campesinos finally have firm roofs and floors, a health clinic, a doctor; they send their children to school and care for them. The poor didn't have to beg for all of this. They acquired it by working for more just wages. This is the only way to build durable relationships and fair exchanges.

Ethics Attack

For having taken the weak out of misery, Fairtrade is one of the few economic initiatives that has demonstrated its validity. It is also a real alternative to the neoliberal model which it challenges and tries to correct its excesses. This different form of commerce was born in the state of Oaxaca, Mexico, where a group of coffee-producing campesinos came together to form an independent organization, the Union of Indigenous Communities of the Isthmus Region, or UCIRI, to obtain a more fair price for their organic coffee production. The small producers, who were exploited by lawless and faithless intermediaries, organized themselves so that the selling price of their production integrated all of the costs incurred, including social and environmental costs. Fairtrade seeks to pay a fair price to campesinos, and this means paying for investment, their hours of labour, as well as a price for maintaining the environment and their social structures. For more than thirty years, I have helped the indigenous peoples of Mexico to learn about their rights and especially their right to self-organization of work. That is why I prompted them to organize in cooperatives and defend themselves. This is how the members of UCIRI learned to export their product, coffee, without intermediaries and without the assistance of charity organizations. They learned to draw up their contracts and sell their organic coffee. They fixed a minimum price in advance, to ensure a regular income to farmers. Between 2000 and 2005, when the market price for coffee was at forty-five cents a kilo, this system played an important role as a buffer. They could offer $1.21 per kilo – that's triple! That represents additional earnings of $1 million a year to a small cooperative.

In this way, the earnings of the associated farmers progressed significantly, to the point where they doubled in ten years. They could carry out a number of projects, improve their homes, and transportation, create infrastructure, and develop a microcredit bank. Now they truly feel like owners, responsible and with a much less uncertain future. Another fundamental aspect of Fairtrade is the democratic organization of cooperatives in the areas of management and control by the campesinos themselves.

I created the first Fairtrade certification label in 1989 in Holland, under the name Max Havelaar,[3] with a friend, Niko Roozen. Later, the phenomenon developed in dozens of other countries, with the objective of creating and developing a market that included all of those responsible: producers, consumers and industry. This is how we advanced from protests against an unfair market to a true, concrete alternative, the approach of Fairtrade. To resign ourselves to protest alone will be in vain, if we don't have concrete solutions in order to change the situation.

---

[3]   Max Havelaar: named after a fictional character in a 19th century Dutch
      novel of the same name which was very critical of Dutch colonialism.

It is a revolution, but a peaceful one that rests on a constructive proposal that challenges the system based on wealth and the dominant. The producers demand and fight for another type of market, another economy, where volume and wealth are not the only motives. They are seeking an economy that takes into account the dignity of all actors in the chain. All of the rules of this new market should achieve this basic principle. That is why the fair market is not only a fundamental critic of the neoliberal system, but it also offers an alternative economic paradigm.

The idea of a fair market, whose products are of high quality and are sold at a fixed price that integrates a premium for social justice and the protection of the environment arose from the idea of a new economy where campesinos, small producers and workers

are all compensated in the same way for their efforts (hours and sweat) when producing a good. Normally multi-millionaires, politicians and officials receive a salary according to the position they occupy and not according to what they produce, or what would be considered fair compensation. The fair market has been designed so that all of this changes and that remuneration is proportionate to agreed efforts, but also so that preference is given to organic products that respect the environment, the earth, the rivers, the air and the oceans. As Oscar Lafontaine said, "It is the heart of Fairtrade, and that heart beats on the left side."

Fairtrade, in its most generous sense, allows everyone to rise from misery and live with dignity, not become rich. Fairtrade benefits the members of a community, but also the entire surrounding population. The principles of the fair market are viable alternatives to create a new system where each and every person has his/her place, has access to healthcare, school, earnings and work. The neoliberal market model manufactures exclusion, and only the strongest can survive in this extremely competitive universe. That is why, twenty-some years ago, we began to develop a different market that modifies and corrects the large failures of the neoliberal system.

The aim of this market is to create social and solidarity enterprises at a global level, in cooperation with conscious and responsible consumers. To speak of the social and solidarity economy doesn't mean just having compassion for the dispossessed; it means understanding their way of life and having respect for them. Confronted with a rapacious economy that excludes them, they constructed a more equitable distribution system that includes them.

If we forget this, we rely solely on the dominant system to try to erase its own negative aspects through means like charity. That is the reason why the solidarity economy should opt for a different dimension and in the future propose things from a much broader point of view – because the very essence of humankind is multidimensional and not only oriented to profit. It was a grave error of singular, mathematical and scientific thought to believe the inverse.

Fairtrade is the establishment of an alternative of compassion and recognition in a society where those values are becoming absent. Not for moral reasons, but out of simple respect for human beings. Fairtrade created the conditions that allowed a little bit of happiness to arise on this earth – real, not supposed happiness, like the kind promoted by consumer society encouraging purchasing and the accumulation of wealth. For this reason, Fairtrade is a fundamental correction to the dominant capitalist system. Capitalism produces its own hell, but not in the 'afterlife' or 'the others', as Sartre said. It is here on earth.

Fairtrade creates the conditions of solidarity and recognition, of empathy. Like another world – a place of hope and survival – it is a human laboratory to envisage how the most impoverished people can get ahead. It is a place where the manufacture of victims, of the poor and abandoned, is limited as much as possible. It is a pleasant world with less conflict. And it comes from below, mobilizing the common sense and spirit of the poor. They never give up, and they defend what is vital to them. Every human being wants to survive unless his/her rationality has been altered.

Buying Fairtrade products is a vote with your wallet for another world, and in doing so, recognizes that it is possible. Fairtrade is not charity in disguise. It has been designed for both producers and consumers. It is a constructive choice. Luckily, those who have grown tired of not knowing where the money from charity campaigns goes from now on have a tool for this. Many people dislike the Charity Business and Fairtrade offers an alternative to those who would like to do something, like construct a fair world. This implies honesty from one extreme in the chain to the other. And, if the consumer is in doubt of the honesty of the whole Fairtrade chain, the system could fall apart.

And it Works!

We have learned a lot since the beginnings of Fairtrade. True, many things can still be improved. However, among the positive consequences are the capacity of campesinos to organize themselves in communities, recover their dignity, the return of political rights, social structure and the 100% increase in earnings of indigenous peoples. Earnings rose from one to two dollars per day, and this is the highest it has ever been, although it is still too little.

The organization of campesino communities has created the conditions for a more dignified survival that has permitted them to better resist the crisis. The social projects, and improvements that they have undertaken in the last ten years, the roads created by authorities, the establishment of health centres, the creation of cooperatives so that they could pay less for basic, indispensable goods, means that the campesinos have been less susceptible to the muzzle of capitalism. Now, basic goods are readily available for even the poorest. Prior to working with Fairtrade, they had to walk one or two days to get them. At the same time, they are able to sell their harvest at higher prices. In a period of intense crisis like the one we are now experiencing, Fairtrade serves as a buffer for the most dispossessed.

We have also developed a micro-credit cooperative with the money of the members of the organization. The community members administer the cooperative themselves, it is not manna that is imposed from above. There is real progress on the earth, although it may not qualify as true economic development by usual economic standards.

Culture, solidarity and social themes have progressed, as well as technical knowledge, rights and production. This is all due to the efforts of the collectively-organized indigenous peoples. Together they achieve things that they never would have imagined doing by themselves. The recognition of small producers at the political level also comes from this progress. Twenty years ago, indigenous people were considered to be animals, even in the nearby cities. Today, the entire world knows what these campesinos have achieved and its significance. Their products are in supermarket stands in all of the western countries and the quality of their production is renowned. These people who lived in misery have taken their

Francisco Van der Hoff in front of the magnificent mural at Just Us! Coffee Roasters Co-op done by UCIRI artist Raúl Guzmán Enriquez, titled *'Comercio sin Sangre de Explotación'* (Trade without the Blood of Exploitation).

At Francisco's small coffee farm in Buena Vista, high in the mountains of Oaxaca, telling a visitor from Just Us! about his coffee plants.

Panel on the Future of Fairtrade in 2005 at the opening of the Fairtrade Museum in Grand Pré, Nova Scotia. (l-r) Carolyn Whitby (Fairtrade Canada), Jonathan Rosenthal (co-founder, Equal Exchange, Boston), Brian O'Neil (Oxfam Canada), Francisco, Isabelle St-Germain and Normand Roy (co-founders, Equiterre, Montreal)

Francisco in his small one-room house in Oaxaca. His needs are simple, but he does now count the Internet among his necessities. It connects him and the UCIRI co-op with the world.

Organic coffee farming is hard and unpredictable, but can be rewarding and enjoyable. UCIRI member Enan Eduardo Lopez with his daughter Tañia picking coffee cherries.

Guadalupe Echevarria, who, with her husband Manuel Iglesias, was one of the founders of UCIRI. Being born a twin, it was assumed she would take on the role of community healer, which she has done for most of her long and healthy life.

Guadalupe and her community of Chayotepec have been charged with protecting an old growth rainforest and have consequently developed a successful eco-tourism project to complement their coffee production.

Walking is a big part of everyday life in the mountains – to coffee plots, to visit distant neighbours and to attend regular co-op meetings.

Fairtrade co-ops knew from the start that they had to emphasize quality in addition to the social and environmental benefits. Here, members of the CASIL Co-op (Northern Peru) are 'cupping' or evaluating their latest crop.

UCIRI has generously supported other Fairtrade co-ops like ASOBAGRI in Barrillas, Guatemala who are now known globally for their fine coffee.

Fairtrade quickly moved beyond just coffee to include tea, chocolate, sugar, bananas, etc. Here are Maria Guzman and Margarita Borja from the Jambi Kiwa Co-op in Riobamba, Ecuador checking the weight of Margarita's herbs before they go for processing and packaging in their own herbal tea factory.

Oromia, a coffee growing area in southwestern Ethiopia is actually the birthplace of coffee. Coffee has become the second most traded commodity in the world next to oil. Many fortunes have been made from coffee, yet the small farmers who grow most of our coffee remain desperately poor.

The Oromia Coffee Farmers Co-operative Union is owned by over 200,000 small farmers in 217 member co-operatives. They have been able to develop their own production infra-structure which includes coffee washing and sun drying stations (shown on right) and a very impressive processing plant near the capital, Addis Ababa.

The needs of the Oromia communities are so great and so basic. The farmers, themselves, meet to decide their priorities, which have generally fallen into the categories of education (at all levels), health clinics, clean water and transportation.

BioFach, Nurnberg is the world's largest organic trade show and conference. It is a great place for both Fairtrade co-ops and buyers to meet many of their current and potential trading partners in one place. Here Jeff Moore (centre) of Just Us! meets with Barend Salomo (right), chair of the Wupperthal Rooibos Tea Co-op in South Africa and Charles Darling (left) of Fair Packers, a packaging factory they co-own.

At this members meeting of the Wupperthal Rooibos Tea Co-op, members were sharing their stories and struggles. They explained that the white South African farmers can have farms of thousands of hectares, much of their land unused, while it is virtually impossible for black farmers to buy even a tiny plot. Fortunately the co-op was given their land by a church. The man in the foreground explained that even though being a member of the co-op involved more work and more risk, he could never go back to the humilation he experienced working on plantations.

Fairtrade has also developed in Asia, but the model is somewhat compromised, as it is in South Africa and elsewhere, because of the colonial history. Here in Darjeeling, the tea pickers can organize into co-operatives of workers on plantations even though they don't own the land or factory. They may negotiate benefits such as daycare (background) and other working and living conditions, but it is often incremental rather than transformative change.

At its heart, Fairtrade is not just meant to bring a better income. More importantly it is about democratic participation, leadership development, dignity and greater control over their own destinies. It is meant to be tranformative, moving small producers out of neo-colonial structures to a qualitatively better future.

Fairtrade has really caught on for both producers and consumers who have seen that they can actually effect change from below. With its growth, however, Fairtrade has become all things to all people. The original intent of improving the lives of small producers is in danger of being lost. Hence the introduction in 2011 of the Small Producers Symbol, owned and managed by small producers themselves under an independent foundation, FUNDEPPO (Foundation of Organized Small Producers). See www.spp.coop

Small producers and traders came together in true solidarity to take Fairtrade to another level. The Small Producers Symbol proudly and clearly distinguishes products from organized small producers for both domestic and export markets. It ensures consumers of quality products, grown sustainably, which contribute to building the strength, dignity and well-being of small producers and their communities, now and in the future.

destiny into their own hands, and with dignity, have become true economic actors. With this energy, they organized, and little by little, they grew more confident in their own abilities. This is how they adapt, more and more every day, to the world that surrounds them. Prior to this, they waited for the system to resolve their problems. Fairtrade gave them the means to win true autonomy – economic, cultural and political.

That is what Subcommandante Marcos tried to do in Chiapas. In the Zapatista uprising of the mid 90s he arose to say, "We are indigenous and ancestral inhabitants of this country. We are citizens with full rights and at the same time we are indigenous." However, Mexico, like many other countries, is not truly a pluricultural society, and as such, failed to perceive value in the diversity of the inhabitants of Chiapas and continued to treat them as an insignificant number. Nonetheless, we all form a part of the same society.

This is the principle demand of 'zapatismo'. It should not be seen as a struggle of the minorities to take power. Rather, it is the will to live like others and have the same rights. We were in contact with them. Ultimately, it is the same struggle, but by different means. As with Gandhi, I believe in non-violence. I have never thought of armed resistance as a good thing. The recognition of diversity is the best way to avoid conflicts. Without it, we provoke violence. When society does not recognize one or the other, it creates frustrations. Options imposed from above, for example the creation of Israel by the British to the detriment of the abandoned Palestinians, creates imbalance. The British abandoned the game when the conflict began between Israel and the Palestinians, who were the original inhabitants of the land. It is an insult to rationality. It makes solving the problem extremely difficult, if not impossible, because there was denial of one of the parties. This is how victimization of the scapegoat[4] originates, essential to the whole dynamic. The poor form part of this victimization mechanism and their demands now threaten the dominant society.

The Devil is Dressed as a Multinational

At the start of Fairtrade, we were allied with the traditional, alternative market – small stores and a few small coffee companies that were under the same pressure to continue in the market. These are creative and reactive partnerships that try to fight the large companies with intelligence. When we launched Fairtrade certification in Holland at the end of the 1980s, we immediately saw the reaction of the multinationals, who arrogantly believed in capitalism, and were organized like the mafia, as they tried to block our way. These multinationals threatened to cancel the orders of the small coffee roaster who wanted to work with us.

Fortunately, there are businessmen and family-run companies in the larger world that are conscious of the need to share the wealth and produce without harming the environment. However, what is possible for small businesses on a human scale is impossible for the multinationals whose investors are the ones that make the key decisions. The only thing that motivates them is the limitless growth of profit, efficiency and power. Small companies don't have this burden. They are more audacious, can take risks, and in certain cases, are more efficient than large companies. When Nestlé or other multinational corporations like Kraft assure us that 1% of their products are Fairtrade, in reality it is for publicity

---

[4]   Victimization of the scapegoat: the theory developed by Rene Girard on origins of violence.

purposes to promote the other 99% of their regular activities. When they come to visit us, it is to use us as a smokescreen. We favour a different kind of distribution of profit. We are not against profit. There are many examples in the world of companies where co-ownership of employees by means of shares in the company is highly developed and it works.

As is natural, our job is to have mutual understanding with the small actors constantly threatened by bigger actors, facing the possibility of losing the little that we have. This can only work it seems, with small and medium-sized partners. The big companies, blinded by their market share, their pride and power, cannot imagine that innovations come from some other source. We are not against multinationals, as we have always been open to working with the distributors, even when it comes to multinational corporations. This excludes, however, Nestlé, Kraft, Sara Lee, Procter and Gamble, Dreyfus and Ecom. They exploit primary resources at low cost and sell them directly with profit margins on the backs of the producers. The same ones who accused Fairtrade of distorting the markets with a minimum guaranteed price for coffee, such as Nestlé, then did everything they could to obtain the Max Havelaar or Fairtrade label. From the moment Fairtrade achieved a market share of 2-3%, their objective was to infiltrate the system and to observe from the inside. Once they had done that, they created their own ecological brand inspired by the ideas of Fairtrade without respecting its foundations. For the multinationals, Max Havelaar upset the market and imposed price hikes. Since they could not oppose the success of Max Havelaar, they diverted the system to create their own certification with practically no extra cost for them. It is unthinkable for a multinational that a small equitable market could challenge the laws of the system. They can't stand that the coffee of small producers represents 5% of today's coffee market. In order for this to change, the devil had to be converted. As I know the functioning of multinational corporations, I say that this still has to happen! In order for this to change, politicians, shareholders and managerial structures of corporations also have to change. If and how that all will happen remains to be seen.

The Little Philosophy of the Poor

Luckily, there is hope in the values conveyed by the poor, those from below, the disinherited. The campesinos and the abandoned of the entire world possess a different culture, set apart from the western stereotypes and the values that embody cities and consumer society. They cannot be pigeonholed by modern society. In a way, they are somewhat pre-modern, original. On the other hand, when campesinos visit western societies, they feel bad. So much affluence makes them uncomfortable. They feel better in a rural, traditional system that is more human, more respectful of people, and with less anonymity. In the developed cities, they feel like animals in a carnival-like environment, a kind of zoo. "In which world are we?" they ask. Their most common response is, "But this is a completely false world!" Particularly if you listen to the people saying "but we must help the poor, show them that another way of life is possible – they must be very miserable even though they live in harmony with nature".

Paradoxically, the exploited are the ones who have made modern society possible. The labour sector was fed from their fields, as well as the productive sector. Nevertheless, contemporary society is afraid of the campesinos, the poor and the abandoned. The worst thing is they are aware of the poverty in the rural areas and the suburbs, and above all, that it is growing. There is a negative bias against the people they consider to be bums, poorly dressed, lacking in good manners, and who also speak a language that is difficult to understand – a dialect or slang.

Over the centuries, the wealth of modernity was squeezed from the poor like juice from a lemon. That is why, at times, campesinos are reluctant to adopt the idea of modernity. With good reason they mistrust this idea of progress that never touches them. It is always some other intermediary that takes advantage of their agricultural products, for example, agents for large coffee corporations or large distribution networks. The campesinos know this. So, they ask where the profits go and look for a way to sell directly, and at a higher price. They do not want to be exploited from above, from the cities, from the north. They depend on a number of cycles of production: the weather, the 'passing of things'. Modernity has not contributed to their development; rather, it has maintained them in a permanent state of vulnerablity or crisis. If they have a bad year, they lose everything. So, the poor do not see what good can come of progress. Campesinos love their land, their produce, their cows – they have an intimate relationship with nature and the world that surrounds them.

However, society is organized to provide cheap agricultural products to the inhabitants of cities to offer food security, and to ensure that the forces of production work. We have to end subsidies and pay a fair price to the producers. In Europe, each cow makes two times more than a Mexican or Brazilian campesino thanks to subsidies! This system was put in place to ensure workers access to raw materials at the lowest possible price to guarantee social peace. Since World War II, farmers have been neglected and kept in an unbearable relationship that could not be worse. However, food comes from the country; therefore, small producers are indispensable to the survival of cities.

There is also pressure from producers of agro-fuels who retain a part of their harvest to fill the tanks of cars. This leads to aberrations. In 2009, Mexico had to import subsidized corn from the USA. Prior to this, the country had long been an exporter of corn. This is happening because cheaper subsidized products can be found in other countries like the USA. On a global scale, it is absurd. The North American Free Trade Agreement made this possible. Local farmers could not compete with this new policy. Nobody has taken the time to calculate the ecological, political or social consequences of this type of policy making. This is the illogicality of the market.

For this reason, we cannot trust the invisible hand that supposedly regulates the market. It does not work; it is a utopia. Isn't there a paradox in the use of food for agro-fuel when millions of people do not have enough to eat, and the producers never see the benefits of their production?

Chapter 3

ANOTHER WORLD IS POSSIBLE

To Oppose is to Propose

The experience of the student movement, above all in Europe in 1968, taught me that protest is meaningless if there is no credible alternative or tangible proposal to remedy the ills of the present. The future is not constructed with cries against all of the problems of the present. That is why I developed this slogan that belongs to my community in Mexico: "We keep protesting, but at the same time we keep proposing." The alternative market, which is different from the conventional market, is an integral part of this protest and propose movement.

In times of crisis, today as always, a profound re-evaluation of the operation of the economy is not only necessary, it is especially urgent. It is essential to ask: "What kind of social economy of the excluded do we want? And, what model of the social economy not only offers survival (albeit threatened) to the millions of poor, but also equally articulates a new economy?" I say again to all, this new beginning exists, although it is not yet known. Yes, the poor know how to produce, survive, struggle, and organize themselves; and their wisdom is, at times, more important than that of the lightweight economic and social scientists. The abilities of the poor are the same as those of the rich. However, these poor 'Bonsai people', as Muhammad Yunus calls them, have a hard time getting out of the little pot where they have been held to limit their growth in awareness.

From the moment the market economy proved its incapability to truly resolve problems, it has been time for some complete rethinking and discipline. The new economic paradigm that we are developing is based on five postulates: the economy serves the people and not the reverse; development is measured with people and not with objects; growth and development are two distinct concepts, and development, precisely, does not necessarily lead to growth; no economic process can take place outside of what ecosystems provide; and, the economy is a subset of a larger, finite and closed system that is the biosphere. Consequently, infinite growth is an impossibility.

It is time that the world recognized the principles that made micro-credit and Fairtrade successful. Voices, up until this point imperceptible, conquered a space to express different ideas. Now it is time to listen and act accordingly. Exit doors out of this global crisis exist. We have found some.

I forged a model that has an intrinsic quality of solidarity based on a social economy, but did not try to impose solidarity – much less charity – in the heart of the system. It is on the margins of the mainstream economy, mainly in the agriculture field of small farmers, that we were able to introduce new types of trade. Together we proved that the poor, the excluded, are not waiting for ready-made solutions, but that they themselves construct their own solutions to their future. It is only under this condition that those who up until this point have felt abandoned by the world market can be actors today and tomorrow.

This concrete materialization of the theory of Fairtrade widely surpasses the framework in which it was created. It does a lot more then creating a market for agricultural products. It reminds us of the image of malaise of western consumer society, its deviations, of the belief in scientific progress that appears to be the 'emissary of a better world!' It sets individuals against economic materialism that is stripped of spirituality, leading society towards a regression that is at once individualist, sectarian and conforming. It questions the entire world on the very basis of current economic theories and their evolution. Over twenty years ago Fairtrade challenged the neoliberal system and tried to reduce its devastating effects. Fairtrade is also a cultural humanizing endeavour. In the process, it has also begun to humanize our global economy.

A new system, essentially social, that would be a new market space based on agreement of all the actors, and could reduce economic servitude, should replace the existing system where the utopia of the markets imposes slavery on so many people. It is in this context that Fairtrade can show the way to a reformulation of the economic system, giving human beings a central place in society, and in democratic and social development. We can modify the terms of trade at the same time that we test a new viable economic space for producers, which is also acceptable for consumers. In a period of crisis, the disorganization of the world economy is insufferable except for those who know how to take advantage. Those that don't call for more solidarity, although they have forged the tools for another viable world where profit and cost effectiveness are not the only values. We do not rebel against the market simply because we are and want to be part of the market. We want a different market – humane, democratic and social. Likewise, we do not rebel against all of the multinationals (only some). We simply are trying to insert ourselves into the market with dignity for all involved and respect for a minimal standard of democracy. We are not looking for a scapegoat: we only want to see the actual system and the laws that govern it evolve.

The Objectives of 'Social Business'

From different political, economic, cultural and social perspectives, since the beginning of the 1980s, Fairtrade has demonstrated success and durability. It is something real and concrete that is broadening in a substantial manner. In effect, today there are more than one million families that benefit from the Fairtrade system. It is with their determination, intelligence and creativity that thousands of people's lives have improved, not with the aid or charity of western countries. Fairtrade has proved this. There is no need for humiliation of the miserable on the one hand or social rebellion on the other side of the spectrum. Global disorders can actually be resolved.

Fairtrade has proven that with better organization of relations between people, a new perception of the world we live in was and is possible. All of those citizens of the world who have re-appropriated their future are the living proof. Finally, the Fairtrade communities made the existence of a connection between social cost, the producer, the environment and the cost of goods possible. It is obvious that the market should serve people and the environment, not the inverse. That is why we went looking for direct allies among consumers.

We will emerge from the crisis and the atmosphere of discouragement in the long term if we adopt this third way and treat the profound causes and not only the symptoms. These are not utopias, but realistic and durable actions that seek to transform the capitalist system from the inside so the world can be a better place – more humane and more just.

The Fairtrade market is no longer a necessary evolution of capitalism; rather, it is an urgent solution. It can be described as revolutionary evolution or post-capitalist. It changes the rules: social cost, environmental cost, the cost of production, and regeneration of the workforce, should, from now on, make up part of the cost of a good or service. This method is based on the implementation of an international system. For this to happen, markets must be opened up to involve as many participants as possible.

An Alternative Current

As Fairtrade advanced, a number of anti-globalization movements emerged. It is possible to build bridges and exchange. With the agony of the capitalist system and the increase of poverty, people are becoming more and more aware of the chaos of the system. There is a compassion growing from the ills that affect the planet and its inhabitants, and because of this, many people are joining organizations because they know that they cannot act alone. All of the disasters and wars taking place move people who eventually become aware that they don't want more of this world – that they are fed up with all this. Everything that governments refuse to do for human beings, now associations, anti-globalization movements, and responsible enterprises increasingly do for them. The collectivity provides its own antidote.

After the 1980s, which were a true failure from this point of view, the 1990s saw a tremendous U-turn. In this respect, Seattle was an important moment for the formation of an international consciousness, and Geneva as well. Each time, more and more people have protested their irritation and annoyance with the imbalances in the world, and the totalitarian institutions that will supposedly fix things, but really embody the problems – for example, the International Monetary Fund and the World Trade Organization. My own social conscience was awakened during the Vietnam War. I found it absurd and this led me to ask many questions. It was the same since the war in Iraq in the early 1990s, to the North American occupation in Afghanistan, and Abu Ghraib. Suddenly, the young and the not-so-young protested their opposition to all of this. European public opinion was clearly against the war in Iraq. This all led to the emergence of different currents that, in the end, demonstrate the same courage. The emergence of Fairtrade as an organized movement also consolidated the idea that other movements, environmentalists, or those in favour of human rights, could exist and strengthen. They are also accompanied by university students who are becoming more interested in Fairtrade in increasing numbers. There are many academic publications of high quality on Fairtrade, from the University of Bologna to Louvain to Toronto, where there is an entire department dedicated to Fairtrade. It is not propaganda because the work comes from independent researchers. The academic world is a very strong engine for the promotion and critical surveillance of Fairtrade.

Above all, it is at the grassroots level that all these movements together have been created in order to recuperate a democracy, stolen by the elites and the powers-that-be. This created a new fertile platform that seeks to strengthen itself over time. A secondary effect also arose: the repression of the expression of critical opinion by plutocratic states that are eager to retain power.

This was accompanied by a broad-based movement that takes into consideration what is at stake at the environmental and social levels. Spokespeople like Al Gore, Michael Moore, Yann Arthus-Bertrand, Nicolas Hulot, among others, are calling for world change, and a change in the rules, and that is a good thing. But in between Greenpeace and Gore there are a large quantity of associations whose objectives do not always converge. Notwithstanding, each time they propose more precise solutions. Little by little they leave behind their scarecrow disguises that only served to warn of the damages caused by capitalism, in order to truly act on real changes and solutions.

For this reason, we must mobilize the alternative good will into a citizen's movement. I believe that each one of us, consumer, Fairtrade actor, must do our homework and play a role. Together, we can ally the support for Fairtrade with that of other organizations, whether they are environmental or social movements. We are all players, consumers or producers. Therefore Greenpeace, the International Federation of Organic Agriculture Movements (IFOAM), the World Wide Fund for Nature (WWF), Fairtrade and the large number of cooperatives that exist in the world should build bridges and ensure that the message gets across. We are natural allies, but these are slow processes.

Muhammad Yunus, for example, did phenomenal work in Bangladesh and other parts of the world. The Grameen Bank and also Grameen Telephone helped in numerous countries. The model is an example. However, I do not agree with his vision of 'social capitalism' as an end point: it is a sweet dream, a utopia. Capitalism and the social are opposed – it is an oxymoron. Micro-credit is essential in the countryside, in the suburbs, but it already existed prior to Yunus. Micro-credit is inseparable from Fairtrade, they are linked. When, thanks to Fairtrade, the people arise from misery, they can think about carrying out projects. We have encouraged the campesinos to invest the profit from their coffee production in a small cooperative bank, where they have capital, and make loans to community members. It is called the 'Bank of Hope' and it functions well. We have a pre-determined interest rate of only 2%. Nonetheless, the fact that Muhammad Yunus had developed the concept is important. He did considerable work in one of the poorest countries in the world, where very few people can obtain a loan from the big banks. Small loans do not interest the big banks. Above all, most of the applicants do not need 100,000 euros, only a small quantity to start a little store, or buy what they need to start their activity. Regardless, Yunus' model, which relies on funds from abroad, and mostly from the west, has its limits. As the bank grows, questions arise about control, transparency and the responsibility regarding the distribution of funds, and its separation from its original strong connection to the communities it serves.

Despite all of the impediments, we must work with all those who, one way or another, take into account humanity, happiness and the human condition. Everyone, even well-meaning labour unions and environmental organizations must be warned against ecological elitism, and bring together all types of organizations from around the world. The radicals did not achieve anything alone. You have to try to bring everyone together in spite of different opinions. First, let's see what unites us, and then we'll see what divides us!

A More Socialized Internet

New technologies allow exchanges that were impossible just ten years ago. Information circulates automatically thanks to the internet and cellular telephones. The events in Iran are a good example. For their part, the anti-globalization activists knew perfectly well how to use the new communications media that can be transformed into a tool to pressure governments and multinationals. They attack mainstream official media channels that reduce citizens to 'nothing or almost nothing'. Today, a broad-based eco-social platform on the internet still does not exist. It would be a great step forward to unite all forces and alternative proposals on one platform that would create a broad space for expression, democracy, and at the same time, encourage something constructive.

The impact of new technologies has a larger effect in the so-called developing countries compared to the countries of the north. This is because of the poor condition of their existing telecommunications infrastructure. Various studies demonstrate this. For example, the rise of digital technology allows agricultural markets in the south to be more efficient. Campesinos who were formerly isolated can find out the variation of prices, get to know buyers, reduce transaction costs and sell their products at a higher price. For example, in Kerala (a state located in the southwest of the Indian peninsula) access to cell phones permitted an increase of 8% in fishermen's earnings. In Mexico, as in other places, the benefits of Fairtrade have allowed organized communities to purchase computers and have access to the internet. This way, they were able to have a clearer idea of price fluctuations for their products in different markets, and find out where their competitors are located. In some cases, like the state of Madhya Pradesh in India, the campesino's earnings increased by 33%. Thanks to technology, access to learning and distance education has also improved the experience of campesinos, along with their knowledge in meteorology, training, information, direct sales and purchases. The development of access to the internet in the most disadvantaged populations is a condition of their survival. This is proof that new technology can contribute much to the disinherited. Even though access to cell phones is easy, as in Haiti – where more than three million of its nine million inhabitants had a cell phone at the time of the last earthquake – it's not necessarily the same case for the internet.

Supplying access to computers and training the poor to use them is a condition, *sine qua non*, of their emancipation. High speed internet in rural areas could be a solution, like it is in southern Haiti, thanks to the benefits of Fairtrade. However, we have to find a sustainable development model to promote the diffusion of new technologies in the poorest areas of the world. Ironically, the materials used for electronic components in new technology come from these countries.

You Have to Believe It to See It

Capitalism rests on blind faith in the system by its followers in the manner of Francis Fukuyama.[5] Conversely, it is our duty to believe that the rules of capitalism can be changed to create a more just and equitable society. In particular, crises are incredible impulses that allow more people to realize how poorly the world functions, and as a result, new ways of operating come to light.

However, I do not believe in the existence of unilateral models. I refute the blandness of singularity. It has to be constantly questioned. Distinct traditions compel the inhabitants of each country and culture to find their own path, a path that is not necessarily exportable. In Bolivia, we saw that another world

---

5   Fukuyama: American political scientist best known for his book *The End of History and the Last Man* (1992).

is possible after the first election of Evo Morales in 2005 -- an indigenous campesino, and leader of rural organizations and the Movement to Socialism (MAS). However, what happened in Bolivia, one of the poorest countries in Latin America, where the majority of inhabitants are indigenous, cannot be replicated in another place. On the other hand, the movement of the people can provide an example and prove to others that they can take their own initiative.

Historically, in Bolivia, the law did not take into account the interests of campesinos or the poor, and the state had surrendered all of its natural and mineral resources to multinationals. The benefits were never distributed to the population. Under the auspices of Evo Morales, the campesinos had a non-violent reaction, and took control of the country through electoral means to change the system. Morales is not a radical, he did not nationalize everything in a violent manner, like the Iranians or the Zimbabweans who put the boots to the multinationals. Instead, he sought better agreements that gave a larger percentage of benefits from the exploitation of petroleum and gas to the state in order to benefit the poorest Bolivians. This all took place in relative peace and the changes were put in place without clashes or fatalities. Morales did not have a top-down approach, but a more democratic approach. In 2006, he organized a referendum to see if the population approved of the measures he wanted to take in their name. What happened in Bolivia almost a decade ago, and continues to develop, is the archetype of the silent revolution, which I believe is the result of a long process.

Morales reformed the constitution through a constituent assembly in order to improve democracy, and so that it came, as it should, from the people, from below. At the same time, they nationalized sub-surface rights and a certain number of assets indispensable to the survival of the country. In fact, the entire country and the state benefit from new forms of implementing more just and equitable policies. Under his presidency, a fourth power has been instituted, that monitors the performance of democracy and the three state powers: the executive, legislative and judicial levels. In a country accustomed to dictatorships, it is a big step toward true democracy. In addition, Morales' ecological concerns are very strong.

In parallel, Morales walks together with the late Hugo Chavez in Venezuela, who, contrary to the image that has been cultivated outside the country, implemented a model quite similar to that of the Bolivian president. Chavez also changed the constitution, and directed the benefits of certain raw materials toward social development, restored land to the campesinos, and turned over certain industries for the workers to run. Because he impacted certain North American interests, he is portrayed as a dangerous revolutionary. It's always the same refrain: when someone wants to kill his dog, he says it has rabies.

Using non-violence to confront an extremely violent, ultra-capitalist society seems like a good strategy to me. Raising the masses is much more politically efficient and morally violent than a confrontation with the risk of bloody repression. This is the tradition of Gandhi and the Indian independence movement. In his memoirs, Mandela explains that, in the beginning, the African National Congress (ANC) was in favour of violence. However, after spending 27 years in prison, he realized it was not a good solution. As well, we have seen that the post-apartheid transition that many feared took place without violence and in a democratic manner.

Gross National Happiness

We have to re-think the world – create new foundations for the economic system; give new form to the key indicators taking into consideration entire parts of humanity that have been abandoned. Can we replace the notion of the creation of wealth with something broader? For example, Bhutan, a small kingdom in the Himalayas, put Gross National Happiness (GNH) in their constitution. It substitutes the Gross National Product (GNP) that is used in every country in the world, to measure the wealth of its citizens. While GNP is a rational idea, pure accounting, the search for happiness is not an absurd concept. The Bhutanese, who do not want to be reduced to numbers that express growth or economic development, base the index on many more elements: the preservation of the environment; the conservation of local culture; responsible governance. The GNH led Bhutan to ban the commercialization of tobacco in their territory because of the prohibitive social costs. This interesting idea of a new way of proposing the concept of prosperity is making its way, bit by bit, into the international level. We would have to develop it further. In 2005, I participated in an international gathering in Canada with the King of Bhutan. It is clear that the experience of Fairtrade is going in this same direction. Measuring human development in a more holistic way means governments will have to give equal importance to economic growth and sustainable development. In order to do this, we need to deliberately abandon short-term economic gains related to the over-exploitation of raw materials, for example, and explore more durable and just modes of growth. As with Fairtrade, the idea of GNH implies a more humanistic focus on problems.

World Regulation from Below

The major disaster of the 15th Conference of the Parties (COP 15) to the United Nations Framework Convention on Climate Change (UNFCCC) is that there was no political will for a more humanistic approach. The UN is the international institution that should take over all of these issues of more durable and just modes of growth, but neither the north nor the multinational corporations want this. When the UN makes decisions that the countries of the north or Europe don't like, they stop paying their share; they do not want the organization to grow, or to have power or money. However, it's the only solution. In the beginning, the UN was supposed to be an institution with the capacity to avoid wars and conflicts. The powerful countries did not give it the political power to succeed, and that is the biggest problem with the UN. It is the only international mechanism where all of the countries should be considered equal. However, it has been reduced to a deliberative body, a consensus-seeker, without the possibility of enforcing viable solutions.

The issue of the environment has multiple implications. Activists choose two directions: there are the deep ecologists, who believe in the maintenance of virgin areas that prohibit the presence of humans; and on the other hand, the social ecologists, a more responsible movement that asks how humans can reasonably cohabit with nature. The latter analyzed the causes of climate change that are certainly linked to the exploitation of natural resources. They are worried about food security and quickly questioned the western development model. They carry a lot of weight in the World Social Forum.

I think what happened in the streets of Copenhagen was frustration - with very reasoned cries calling for the need for profound change to the economic model, as well as a questioning of the market and neoliberalism. The citizens of the world are making very constructive proposals to governments, but they are not listening. Above all, governments seem incapable of making decisions even though it is immediately imperative.

Popular organizations must be an even more concrete propositional power. This means that civil society should take part in the deliberations of the large summits. It is one of the key points needed in order for things to change. The summit meetings cannot be political summits: social activists should participate in future talks like Copenhagen, in Mexico or in other places. Above all they should bring forward experiences and ways out of the current model, like organic agriculture or Fairtrade – there are tons of constructive experiences. Even if they exist at the margins of the system, why couldn't the system recognize them? It is to their advantage. They must take these forces seriously. At times they represent conflicting interests in society.

Humans and nature should learn to live together. The industrialization of a valley has an impact hundreds of kilometers away in the forests. However, the followers of deep ecology are radicals that do not consider the fact that many times, the inhabitants of woodland zones enable the survival of biodiversity because they know the land – it is theirs, and as a consequence they protect it. Removing populations from these regions would be a mistake. In nature in its wild state, lions and elephants live well together. I think that humans and nature can coexist. Human beings can be good regulators and maintain equilibrium in the areas where they live. Humans also have a right to survive. Humans have no less rights than animals – both have rights but one does not have more rights than the other. We must find a balance out of respect for our Mother Earth, as they say here in Mexico. We are not talking about the myth of the 'noble savage'; it is not a romantic notion, but rather one that seeks a model of peaceful coexistence, of respect and mutual benefit.

In parallel, there are intense reflections to understand how to reduce pollution. We all have the right to breathe, and in all parts of the world, from Shanghai to New York, the number of cars and traffic bottlenecks have become suffocating and unsustainable. We cannot, on the one hand, call for the protection of the polar ice caps, and on the other develop polluted, overpopulated megacities that escape all regulation. The state should intervene to create non-polluting public transportation (subways and buses) to control the excess of cars, and at the same time increase the production of non-polluting electrical cars.

In order for this to work, world regulation should come from below. The mobilization must not be weakened. The more public opinion demonstrates and is mobilized in ecological and social forums, the more governments will pay attention to their concerns. This could take years, but it is the only solution. Demonstrate, propose and concretely construct precise solutions with propositions and realistic agendas. Today, I do not see any other solution.

Initially, there were both right and left-wing extremists in these movements – Maoists and fascists. Today, there are more consensuses, notably at the social and ethical levels. However, on the international level, there is no unified ecological movement that is strong enough to impose its vision. Fifteen years have passed since Kyoto, Montreal and Copenhagen. With education, the message gets passed on, but it is still not enough. Children are aware of the environment, they can explain it to their parents, but it will take a generation for the message to really spread and for behaviours to truly change.

Conclusion

I DREAMED OF ANOTHER WORLD

The social economy exists, I found it. It is time for it to be officially recognized and for the broader public to also recognize it as an alternative that challenges the dominant economy. Yes, a world with more solidarity is possible, supported by an ethic of the common good that cares for planet earth and humanity as a whole. No one has the right to appropriate that which belongs to everyone. This means a long-term and responsible use of natural resources. It also requires that we improve the logic of the exploitation of nature and strengthen the relationship that unites the fate of humans and the world they inhabit. This is what many experiences of the social economy began to do with success, especially those within the framework of Fairtrade. They developed according to the principles of organic agriculture and a more just distribution of wealth.

The ideology that guides the social and solidarity economy consists of giving the economy the place it deserves in society. Up until now, it has prevailed everywhere and has dictated the options for humanity. It is time to give human beings back their humanity, and to give the earth back its sacredness. A human being is worth far more than a few euros that can be carried in a wallet or kept in a savings account.

The One Truth does not exist; there are many ways to attain a better world. We have to try all the routes, all the tracks; we cannot disregard any of them. Capitalism, for its part, is a monster of single-minded thought that does not tolerate adjustment or criticism of any kind. With neoliberalism, you can't even raise the issue of correcting errors or recognizing excesses – there is only one way, and that is the way of the market. We should not trust the false pretexts of 'social and environmental responsibility' that the multinationals have suddenly discovered. It is only a veil thrown in the face of the world. In this way, the big corporations try to convince us that they are following a new path, when in reality they are only creating a new, virginal image, without profound change, and exonerating themselves of all social responsibility with respect to their past, present and future actions.

In reality, everything is connected – Fairtrade, the environment, society, politics, economics, and also micro-credit. To deny this is to deny the essence of life and humanity itself. For all of the actors in Fairtrade, the environment is a basic fact. We had this intuition more than twenty years ago, with a number of colleagues in what is now a market, notably of small producers. We cannot produce something that guarantees a fair wage to the campesinos but deteriorates the environment in the long-term. And, the inverse is equally true.

By developing Fairtrade, we attacked social injustices but also the problem of the survival of the planet. Everything is inter-connected. It is savage capitalism that caused all of the pollution – of the earth and of human beings. We are proposing ways to resolve some of the ills that affect us. The responsibility of the next generations is compromised. The movement comes from below. Although it is insufficient, it still advances. It is the poor campesinos, the small producers who organized themselves to change everything, because the model that ultra-liberalism tried to impose on them from above was not for them. Together, we created a new market by enabling an encounter with consumers that shared the same ideas.

Governments will not change their policies willingly. We must obligate them to do it. My experience has proven this – plotting the route and leading by example. When 100,000 people demand something in the streets, they have much more weight than isolated individuals. Consumers can also make their voices heard, as the success of the Max Havelaar label has proven around the world.

I believe in the need to propose, discuss, and continue pushing a movement upward from below. The producers should do it, and the consumers, as well as all those who are incensed by the imbalances of the market, but it is better to do it in an organized manner. It is with this one condition that we will manage to be taken seriously. And, when the economy has taken the right direction for the benefit of all the planet's inhabitants, then the market, well-being of the planet, and the common good of all will follow.

INDEX

Just Us! Centre for Small Farms

Though the problems that face the world are increasingly complex,
the solutions remain embarrassingly simple.
Bill Mollison

Just Us! Coffee Roasters Co-operative has been supporting the global Fairtrade movement for over a decade. The advancement of Fairtrade has been positive and rapid and has evolved, arguably, away from some of its foundational concepts of land sovereignty, ecological farming, and community development. In a recent re-visioning of Just Us!, co-founders Jeff and Debra Moore highlighted that Just Us! was always more than Fairtrade. It was in fact a co-operative that was focussed on the food and the farmers of the global south. Whether it was working with farmers to increase quality of product, to help with organic certification, or to help form co-operative marketing, Just Us! can best be described as an organization 'listening to and working with' farmers.

A recognition that smallholder farms, both globally and locally, hold the most promising solutions to address food sovereignty, food security, land and water usage, and climate change, Just Us! has initiated the Centre for Small Farms and has invited Dr. Av Singh, Organic Specialist with Perennia to hold the Just Us! Chair in Small Farm Sustainability.

Based in Grand Pre, Nova Scotia, the Just Us! Centre for Small Farms believes that a just food system is possible, both at a local and a global level, and that globally a unity and connectedness of small scale farmers, globally, is a prerequisite. Towards that end, the Centre for Small Farms, has employed farmers-in-residence to manage a demonstration farm (The Just Food! Farm) to serve as a 'meeting place' for farmers. The farm will highlight farmer-to-farmer innovations and celebrate traditional knowledge systems, looking to that wisdom to guide solutions for a resilient agriculture. The Just Food! Farm looks to acknowledge the contributions made by the Mi'kmaq, the Acadians, the Planters, and the United Empire Loyalists, with specific interest in the early relationships between the indigenous population and the French colonists.

Using the Spanish proverb, "we make the road by walking" the Just Us! Centre for Small Farms does not want to be prescriptive about what the small-farm community will need to address sustainability. Rather it hopes to provide the venue for farmers to gather, share, plan, and act. More specifically, the Centre hopes to help create a just food system.

More books from Permanent Publications

   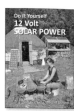 

   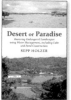 

 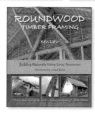